[redacted]

Pebble™

The Calendar

A Day

by Patricia J. Murphy

Consulting Editor: Gail Saunders-Smith, PhD

Capstone press
Mankato, Minnesota

Pebble Books are published by Capstone Press,
151 Good Counsel Drive, P.O. Box 669, Mankato, Minnesota 56002.
www.capstonepress.com

Printed in the United States of America

1 2 3 4 5 6 10 09 08 07 06 05

Library of Congress Cataloging-in-Publication Data
Murphy, Patricia J., 1963–
A day / by Patricia J. Murphy.
p. cm.—(The calendar)
Includes bibliographical references and index.
ISBN 0-7368-3626-8 (hardcover)
1. Calendar—Juvenile literature. 2. Day—Juvenile literature. I. Title.
CE13.M87 2005
529'.1—dc22 2004011900

Summary: Simple text and photographs present information about the parts of a day.

Note to Parents and Teachers

The Calendar set supports national social studies and history standards related to time, place, and change. This book describes and illustrates a day. The images support early readers in understanding the text. The repetition of words and phrases helps early readers learn new words. This book also introduces early readers to subject-specific vocabulary words, which are defined in the Glossary section. Early readers may need assistance to read some words and to use the Table of Contents, Glossary, Read More, Internet Sites, and Index sections of the book.

Table of Contents

TODAY IS...
Sunday
Monday
Tuesday
Wednesday
Thursday
Friday
Saturday
Yesterday
Today
1
2
4
5
6
7

What Is a Day?

A day is 24 hours long. The days of the week are called Sunday, Monday, Tuesday, Wednesday, Thursday, Friday, and Saturday.

The Calendar

January

Sunday	Monday	Tuesday	Wednesday	Thursday	Friday	Saturday
		1	2	3	4	5
6	7	8	9	10	11	12
13	14	15	16	17	18	19
20	21	22	23	24	25	26
27	28	29	30	31		

February

Sunday	Monday	Tuesday	Wednesday	Thursday	Friday	Saturday
					1	2
3	4	5	6	7	8	9
10	11	12	13	14	15	16
17	18	19	20	21	22	23
24	25	26	27	28		

March

Sunday	Monday	Tuesday	Wednesday	Thursday	Friday	Saturday
					1	2
3	4	5	6	7	8	9
10	11	12	13	14	15	16
17	18	19	20	21	22	23
24/31	25	26	27	28	29	30

April

Sunday	Monday	Tuesday	Wednesday	Thursday	Friday	Saturday
	1	2	3	4	5	6
7	8	9	10	11	12	13
14	15	16	17	18	19	20
21	22	23	24	25	26	27
28	29	30				

May

Sunday	Monday	Tuesday	Wednesday	Thursday	Friday	Saturday
			1	2	3	4
5	6	7	8	9	10	11
12	13	14	15	16	17	18
19	20	21	22	23	24	25
26	27	28	29	30	31	

June

Sunday	Monday	Tuesday	Wednesday	Thursday	Friday	Saturday
						1
2	3	4	5	6	7	8
9	10	11	12	13	14	15
16	17	18	19	20	21	22
23/30	24	25	26	27	28	29

July

Sunday	Monday	Tuesday	Wednesday	Thursday	Friday	Saturday
	1	2	3	4	5	6
7	8	9	10	11	12	13
14	15	16	17	18	19	20
21	22	23	24	25	26	27
28	29	30	31			

August

Sunday	Monday	Tuesday	Wednesday	Thursday	Friday	Saturday
				1	2	3
4	5	6	7	8	9	10
11	12	13	14	15	16	17
18	19	20	21	22	23	24
25	26	27	28	29	30	31

September

Sunday	Monday	Tuesday	Wednesday	Thursday	Friday	Saturday
1	2	3	4	5	6	7
8	9	10	11	12	13	14
15	16	17	18	19	20	21
22	23	24	25	26	27	28
29	30					

October

Sunday	Monday	Tuesday	Wednesday	Thursday	Friday	Saturday
		1	2	3	4	5
6	7	8	9	10	11	12
13	14	15	16	17	18	19
20	21	22	23	24	25	26
27	28	29	30	31		

November

Sunday	Monday	Tuesday	Wednesday	Thursday	Friday	Saturday
					1	2
3	4	5	6	7	8	9
10	11	12	13	14	15	16
17	18	19	20	21	22	23
24	25	26	27	28	29	30

December

Sunday	Monday	Tuesday	Wednesday	Thursday	Friday	Saturday
1	2	3	4	5	6	7
8	9	10	11	12	13	14
15	16	17	18	19	20	21
22	23	24	25	26	27	28
29	30	31				

The calendar shows that
one week has seven days.
One month has
28 to 31 days.
One year has 365 days.

Morning

Each day begins
early in the morning.
Nina wakes up
at 7:00.

Nina gets ready
for school.
She eats breakfast
at 7:30.

Elephants
and Their
Calves

At school, Nina reads
a book at 10:00.

Noon is 12:00
in the middle
of the day.
Nina eats lunch
with her friends.

WELLS

Afternoon

At 3:30 in the afternoon,
Nina plays soccer.
She learns to pass
and score.

Evening

At 6:00 in the evening,
Nina and her family
eat supper.
They talk about
their day.

Nina goes to sleep
at 8:00 at night.
The day ends
at midnight.
A new day starts.

Glossary

afternoon—the time of day between noon and evening

calendar—a chart that shows all of the days, weeks, and months in a year; some calendars show one day, one week, or one month at a time.

evening—the time of day between the late afternoon and the early part of the night

hour—a unit of time that equals 60 minutes

midnight—12:00 in the middle of the night; one day ends and another day begins at midnight.

month—one of the 12 parts that make up one year

noon—12:00 in the middle of the day

year—a period of 12 months; the year begins on January 1 and ends on December 31.

Read More

Ganeri, Anita. *Day and Night.* Nature's Patterns. Chicago: Heinemann Library, 2004.

Hughes, Monica. *First Day at School.* Raintree Sprouts. Chicago: Raintree, 2004.

Nelson, Robin. *A Day.* First Step Nonfiction. Minneapolis: Lerner, 2002.

Internet Sites

FactHound offers a safe, fun way to find Internet sites related to this book. All of the sites on FactHound have been researched by our staff.

Here's how:

1. Visit *www.facthound.com*
2. Type in this special code **0736836268** for age-appropriate sites. Or enter a search word related to this book for a more general search.
3. Click on the **Fetch It** button.

FactHound will fetch the best sites for you!

Index

Word Count: 134
Grade: 1
Early-Intervention Level: 10

Editorial Credits
Sarah L. Schuette, editor; Jennifer Bergstrom, set designer

Photo Credits
All photographs by James Photography/James Menk